Distinguished Wisdom Presents . . .

"The Earth Is Sad, Little Timmy"

Pastor Terrance Levise Turner, MBA

Well Spoken Inc. | Nashville, TN

© 2020 Terrance Levise Turner

All rights reserved. No part of this publication may be reproduced, scanned, transmitted or distributed in any printed or electronic or mechanical forms or methods, including photocopying, recording, or other without prior written permission of the publisher, except in the case of brief select quotations embodied in critical reviews and certain other noncommercial uses permitted by copyright law. For permission requests, write to the publisher, addressed below. Unless otherwise indicated, all Scripture quotations are taken from the King James Version of the Bible.

Pastor Terrance Levise Turner.
Well Spoken Inc.
P.O. Box 291806 Nashville, TN. 37229
WellSpokenInc@bellsouth.net
www.TerranceTurnerLivingProverbs.com
Ordering Information

Quantity sales. Special discounts are available on quantity purchases by corporations, associations, and others. For details, contact the "Special Sales Department" at the address above.
Cover design and illustrations by Bambi of
3AM31/99Designs/Terrance Levise Turner
Book design by Terrance Levise Turner
Printed in the United States of America

ISBN: 978-1-733979672 Paperback
ISBN: 978-1-733979689   E-Book
ISBN: 978-1-733979696 Audiobook

Table of Contents

"The Earth is Sad, Little Timmy"..2
The Scientific Explanation Of Earthquakes........................47
    First of all, "What is an Earthquake?"... 47
    Why do we have earthquakes?.. 47
    Earthquakes causes the Earth to "shake"... 48
    How do we know how big an earthquake is?..................................... 48
    Can we know if an earthquake is coming?... 48
Salvation Prayer..50
About The Author..53

This book is dedicated to young people of today and in future generations. I desire that they have a solid understanding of God and His principles for life; and thereby have a successful, prosperous, safe, and godly life.

Also by Pastor Terrance Levise Turner, MBA:

Distinguished Wisdom Presents . . . Living Proverbs–Volume 1

Distinguished Wisdom Presents . . . Living Proverbs–Volume 2

Distinguished Wisdom Presents . . . Living Proverbs–Volume 3

Distinguished Wisdom Presents . . . Living Proverbs–Volume 4

Distinguished Wisdom Presents . . . Living Proverb–Volume 5

Distinguished Wisdom Presents . . . The Dynamic Victory Confession: Powerful Confessions For A Victorious Life!

Distinguished Wisdom Presents . . . Your Wealth Is In Your Anointing: Discover Keys To Releasing Your Potential.

Distinguished Wisdom Presents . . . Gain 20/20 Vision For The New Decade! A Step By Step Path To A More Successful Future.

"The Earth is Sad, Little Timmy"

One day in 1999 after a big earthquake in Taiwan, 8-year-old Little Timmy Johnson's parents took him to see his grandfather. The Johnson's lived in a small city in Tennessee called Wallaceville. Little Timmy's grandfather lived in a special home there for older people. Little Timmy loved his grandfather, and was always excited about seeing him. His plump brown face would brighten whenever his parents told him they were going for a visit. Little Timmy's family first stated calling him "Little Timmy", and because he was the shortest boy at his school, everyone else did too.

When the Johnsons got there Little Timmy was the first one out of the car. He knew exactly where his grandfather's room was. His parents followed as Little Timmy joyfully walked into his grandfather's room. His grandfather sat with his eyes closed. Little Timmy walked up and said, "Hey Granddaddy."

"Hello my little buddy," Little Timmy's grandfather said with a smile.

Little Timmy's parents knew he loved talking with his grandfather so after hugging him and talking a while his parents left so they could talk. Little Timmy had been quiet in the car. He had something on his mind.

"Granddaddy," Little Timmy said, "Why do we have earthquakes?"

Little Timmy's grandfather knew by the unusual question, his grandson had heard about the earthquake in Taiwan. His grandfather had heard about it on the radio the day it happened.

Little Timmy's grandfather was a preacher. He was 89 years old, and Little Timmy thought he was the smartest man in the world. He had all white hair like curly soft wool. His skin was shiny and brown. He had happy wrinkles around his eyes, and mouth. Little Timmy heard the church members say he got those from praying and smiling. He sat near the window in his room so he could feel the sun shining in. He had lost eyesight two years after Little Timmy was born.

Hearing the concern in Little Timmy's voice, Little Timmy's grandfather reached out and pulled him closer. With his big hands on his shoulders, Little Timmy's grandfather said slowly, "The earth is sad, Little Timmy."

Little Timmy looked at his grandfather's gray eyes curiously, and asked, "What made the earth sad, Granddaddy?"

"People son, long time ago," his grandfather said.

"What did people do to make the earth sad, Granddaddy?"

"My little buddy, Granddaddy's going to tell you a story."

Though Little Timmy's grandfather was an old man, he could remember and tell long stories. Little Timmy's plump round face, though still concerned, became happy when his grandfather said he was going to tell a story. He sat up on the bed close to his grandfather's chair.

"Long time ago before all buildings and cars, before streets or anything on them, two people lived on the whole wide earth. God made them."

His grandfather stopped, felt for Little Timmy's hand and grabbed it gently with his, and said, "Little Timmy son, you do remember what you learned about God?"

Little Timmy's face brightened up and he said, "Yes sir, Granddaddy, I remember. He's the biggest, oldest, strongest person all around and He loves me."

"That's right my son, you remember," his grandfather said with a proud smile.

"Before God made people he made the earth, the sky, and the big waters called the seas. Now there was nothing in them so he made something to put in them. God just said, 'Let grass and trees, birds and fish, cows and horses, crickets and frogs, and every kind of thing big and small just come up!'"

Little Timmy's eyes were now big with excitement. He then asked his grandfather curiously, "But where did they come from Granddaddy?"

His grandfather thought a moment. He then said, "God has a special place where he keeps all kinds of good things, and that's where they came from, little buddy."

As Little Timmy's grandfather and he sat about to continue the story a woman walked into the room wearing white clothes and pushing a cart. She had a bowl of green Jell-O, a sandwich, soup and apple juice in a clear plastic cup.

"Hello, Mr. Johnson. I've brought your lunch," she said as she rolled the cart close to him. "And who is this", she said. She patted Little Timmy lightly on the back.

"Ann, this is Little Timmy, my grand boy came to see me today."

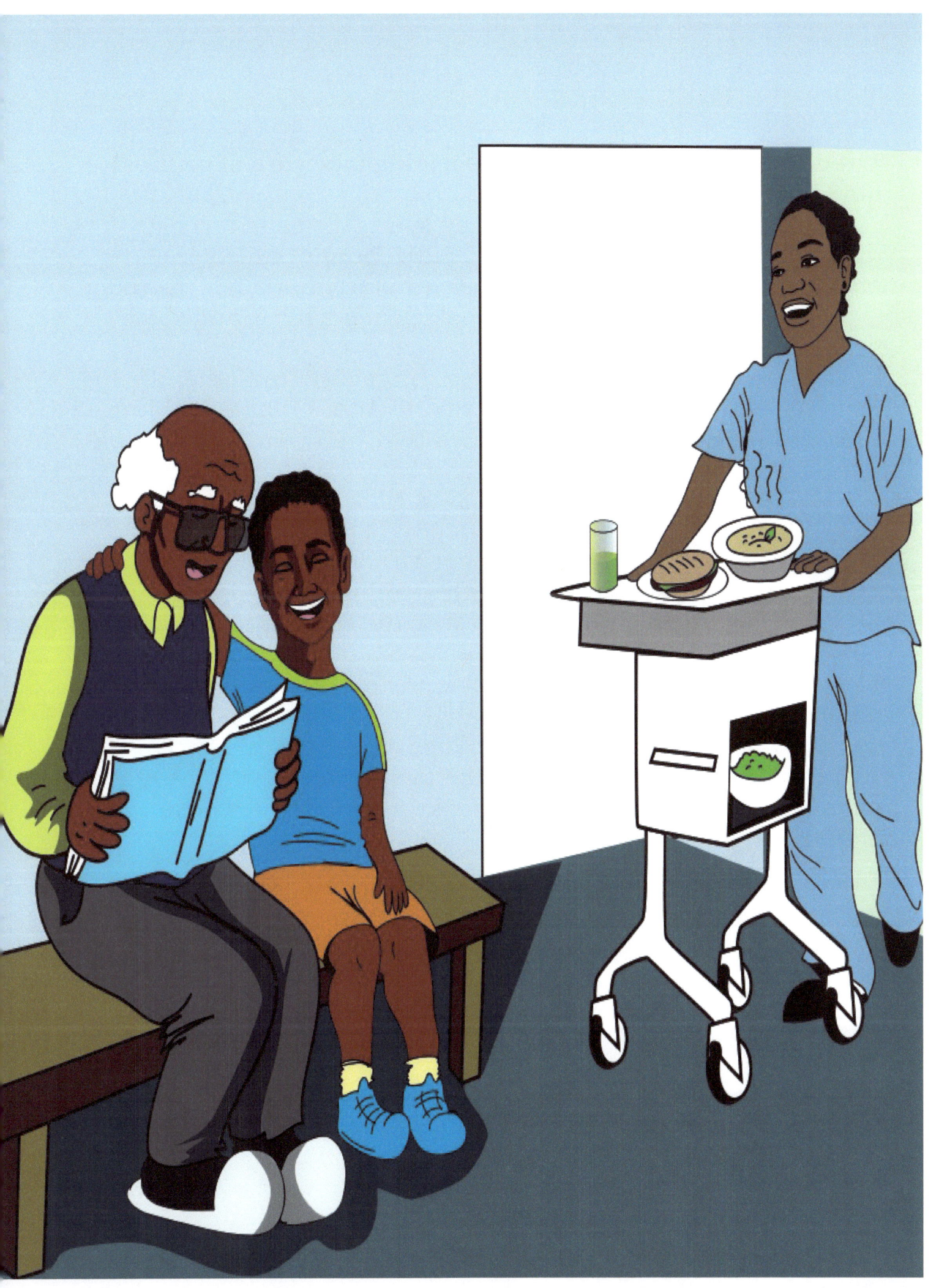

"Little Timmy, Ann has only been helping take care of your old granddaddy a week now."

"Well, let me go get Little Timmy some juice and a cookie. Would you like that Little Timmy?" Little Timmy smiled and nodded. Ann helped his grandfather get started and left the room.

She soon returned with two cookies in a saucer and some apple juice.

Ann stood and watched as Little Timmy's grandfather ate his meal. After finishing most of it he said to Ann, "Thank you, Ann. I think Little Timmy and I both needed that." She smiled and took their dishes. Little Timmy smiled, and said, "Thank you."

After Ann left, Little Timmy moved close to his grandfather again. "She had pretty hair Granddaddy," Little Timmy said.

"And she was nice too wasn't she Grandson?"

"Yes sir," Little Timmy said with a smile.

"Now, let me finish telling you why the earth is sad Grandson. The earth was happy in the beginning. Everything was beautiful. Rivers and streams filled it, and all kinds of trees. Lush peach trees and pear trees, apple trees and orange trees, and even big banana trees. All the animals were happy. They all got along. Everything was peaceful. Even the lions and the tigers played with the other animals. God then said he would make a man and a woman, Adam and Eve.

He would let them be in control of all the animals, trees and land."

"Did the animals, trees and land like man, Granddaddy?"

"Oh yes, they liked him at first. They like him so much that they let him name all of them. "Did you know that?"

"No sir. He must have been smart."

"Yes son. Man was smart. But one day Eve and he did something that was really bad."

"Is that what made the earth sad Granddaddy?"

"Yes Little Timmy," his grandfather said. "They disobeyed God. When God first created Adam and Eve, He made a beautiful garden full of everything they wanted. He told them to enjoy it and to keep it looking beautiful. He told them they could eat anything in the garden. There were all kinds of trees in the garden with all kinds of fruit and good things for them to eat to be healthy and strong. But one tree God said not to eat from. If they ate from this tree, bad things would happen to them."

Little Timmy's grandfather stopped and rested. He then reached into his sweater pocket and pulled out two pieces of butterscotch candy, one for him and one for Little Timmy.

"Little Timmy," his grandfather said, "the tree that God told them not to eat from looked good to them. There was a sneaky snake, the devil that lied to them. He told them they could eat from the tree. He tricked them, and they disobeyed God and ate from the tree."

Little Timmy sat quietly for a moment. He knew that when he disobeyed his parents he got into big trouble. So, he slowly asked, "What happened Granddaddy?"

"Well, you know how your parents have to spank you or take away your toys when you disobey them?"

Little Timmy answered, "Yes sir."

"Well son, God had to discipline Adam and Eve. Because they disobeyed him, he had to make them leave the garden. Also because of them God said the ground of the whole wide earth would be cursed."

Little Timmy's grandfather stopped, and felt for his hand again.

"Little Timmy," he said, "do you know what cursed means?"

Little Timmy quickly answered, "Yes sir, Granddaddy. Anthony Jamison does it all the time on the playground at school, but I don't. Mama told me I should never talk like that. She said if you're not smart enough to say something good you should be quiet."

Little Timmy's grandfather just smiled at first. Then he explained that God was not talking about quite that kind of a curse.

"Little Timmy," he said, "when God says something is cursed that means something bad is going to happen to it. Because Adam and Eve had disobeyed him, God had to let bad things happen to them. They were in control of the earth so bad things happened to the earth too because of them. You see little buddy when we do something wrong it can cause trouble for more than just us."

Little Timmy thought about that a moment. He remembered the times his cousin Mike and he both got into trouble for something only one of them had done. Mike was one year older than Little Timmy and was like a brother to him. Little Timmy didn't have any brothers or sisters, but Mike and he had a lot of fun.

"What happened to the earth Granddaddy?" Little Timmy asked.

Little Timmy's grandfather put his hand on his chin and thought for a moment. He then suddenly raised his hand pointing at Little Timmy, and asked, "Little Timmy, do you remember last year your father, Mike, and you went out into the country and picked your old granddaddy those big sweet blackberries?"

"Yes sir, I remember Granddaddy. That was hard, but it was fun though." Little Timmy said.

"Well, do you remember all of the weeds and stickers growing around there?" His grandfather asked.

"I remember," Little Timmy said. "And I was kinda' scared, 'cause Mike said we were going to see a snake in there."

His grandfather laughed.

"And Granddaddy those stickers tore my hands up."

"Those weeds and stickers are what happened when the earth was cursed little buddy. Before the curse everything was beautiful and free, you didn't have to worry about being stuck or a snake hiding in the berries."

Little Timmy's grandfather sat back and rested. Little Timmy sat back a little on the bed too. His grandfather closed his eyes and leaned his head on the back of his chair. Little Timmy sat quietly. He knew his grandfather was praying. Little Timmy's father had told him when he was younger, "Whenever you see Granddaddy close his eyes and get quiet, you be quiet too, because that's when he's talking to God."

    After a little while, Little Timmy's grandfather opened his eyes. Little Timmy's happy brown eyes were excitedly looking at his grandfather. His father also had told him when his grandfather talks to God, God tells him all kinds of good things and makes him wise. So Little Timmy knew the story was going to get even better.

"Granddaddy are the stickers and weeds what makes the earthquakes come?" Little Timmy asked.

"No son," his grandfather answered. "When Adam and Eve disobeyed God, God let the earth get hard. The dirt got dry and just barely soft enough to plant seeds. Adam had to work very hard to grow food. Have you ever planted seeds Little Timmy?"

Little Timmy was getting ready to answer 'No sir,' but he then thought of a time he thought he had.

"Yes sir, I did one time Granddaddy when Mike and I were eating watermelon in his backyard and we spit the seeds on the ground and the next time we were there little plants were growing."

Little Timmy's grandfather laughed. "Heh, heh, heh, heh." He was not talking about planting in quite that way. He then took a deep breath in and out.

"Well, little buddy it wasn't quite that easy for Adam and Eve. They didn't have the rain they needed to help cause the seeds to grow. Before the curse the earth made it's own water, like the dew on the grass in the morning when you walk to school. But after the curse, the ground got very dry and needed more water to stay soft, but it did not rain in those days. The curse made everything bad. The weather was bad for man and the earth. When it was cold, it was too cold for a long time and when it was hot, it was too hot too long. The earth began to break up and move around inside. That is when it started to shake and quake all around. The earth was sad because man had disobeyed God and had also caused it to be cursed."

Little Timmy was sitting listening to his grandfather totally still. It was as if his grandfather had actually been there.

"Little Timmy, the earthquakes are the earth's way of crying because of the curse. Do you understand?"

"I think so Granddaddy," Little Timmy said. "Anthony Jamison cried in class one time and he stomped his feet and shook his arms all around like he was crazy. I guess he gets mad too when he gets sad."

"Well little buddy, that's sort of the way the earth gets too. The earth is still sad because of what Adam and Eve did. It is sad, because men and women today are still disobeying God. And even though the earth gets plenty of rain now it still moves around inside causing earthquakes.

Little Timmy seemed to understand more about earthquakes as he listened to his grandfather. The concern he had at first had left as he listened but as his grandfather sat quiet again the concern slowly came back to his mind.

"Granddaddy," Little Timmy said sadly, " I heard the man on TV say a lot of people died when the earth was sad. Why won't the earth get happy again and stop earth quaking?"

"Little Timmy," his grandfather began to say, then suddenly stopped. They both heard a buzzing sound coming into his room.

Little Timmy looked up and smiled. It was Mrs. James from down the hall riding in on her special wheel chair.

"Hello Brotha' Preacha,'" she said loudly, riding right into the middle of the room.

Little Timmy's grandfather knew she was coming before she ever got there. Mrs. James talked loudly and happily with everyone she met as she rode down the hall.

Little Timmy's grandfather said, "How are you Mrs. James? I heard you coming."

"Oh I'm fine, fine! Brotha' Preacha. The good Lawd let me see anotha' day, and I ain't got no complaints."

"Well, that's a blessing Mrs. James. The Lord takes care of us doesn't he?" Little Timmy's grandfather said with a smile.

"Yes! He does Brotha' Preacha'," Mrs. James said.

"Mrs. James did you see my little grand boy come to see me today?" Little Timmy's grandfather asked.

Little Timmy was sitting patiently waiting for Mrs. James to speak to him. He always liked her because she was nice to him. She had lived many places and had many stories to tell too. Her eyes got big when she talked and her cheeks shook. Little Timmy thought that was funny but he was always glad to see Mrs. James.

"Well, well baby, come give Mrs. James some sugah'."

Little Timmy hopped off the bed, walked over to her and kissed her on the cheek. She gave him a big kiss and hug in her big, soft arms. Little Timmy laughed.

"So what were you doing down here baby with your old granddaddy?" Mrs. James asked.

"Granddaddy was telling me a story about earthquakes." Little Timmy answered.

"Yeah, Brotha' Preacha' that was a crying shame what happened over in Taiwan." Mrs. James said.

"Yes, I'm explaining to my little grand boy why we have earthquakes, Mrs. James."

"Well, it ain't nothin' but the devil. That's what it is Brotha' Preacha', trying to kill as many of us as he kin. I been in earthquakes in California, snowstorms in Detroit and hurricanes down in Mobile and it ain't been nothin' but the good Lawd that's kept me alive. The devil's busy!"

"You're right Mrs. James the devil does affect the earth but we just have to know that the Lord is in control."

"You're right Brotha' Preacha'. Little Timmy you listen to your granddaddy. He'll tell you what's right."

After talking a little longer with Little Timmy's grandfather Mrs. James said, "I better be getting along Brotha' Preacha'."

She said to Little Timmy, "You be good Little Timmy, Mrs. James will see you next time." She spun around in her special wheelchair and buzzed out of the door.

"So Granddaddy is it the devil who causes earthquakes?" Little Timmy asked when Mrs. James left.

"Little Timmy, the devil does all kinds of bad things. Do you remember he tricked Adam and Eve to disobey God? He causes bad things to happen to the earth too. But it all started when Adam and Eve let him trick them into eating the fruit and disobey God. Do you remember?"

"I remember," Little Timmy said.

Little Timmy sat quietly again. He was thinking about all his grandfather had said. He was thinking about what Mrs. James had said. His grandfather could tell Little Timmy had more questions.

Little Timmy's grandfather wanted him to know about earthquakes but also he wanted him to know one day they were going to end. "Little Timmy," he said, "I know you remember what Granddaddy told you about Jesus, God's Son?"

"Yes sir," Little Timmy said, "but which part Granddaddy?"

"The part about him coming from heaven to save us from the bad things we do.

"I remember Granddaddy. He loved the world so he died for us," Little Timmy said happily.

"Yes, that's right. And he rose again and went back to heaven," his grandfather said.

Little Timmy's grandfather sat silently for a moment. He then asked, "Little Timmy, do you still remember the song you learned for Easter?"

"Yes sir," Little Timmy said and he began to sing: "He arose. He arose. He arose from the dead. He arose. He arose. He arose from the dead. He arose…"

"Well yes, that's right Little Timmy and he told us that there would be earthquakes. But do you remember what else he said little buddy?"

Little Timmy thought for a little while and then said, "No sir."

"Jesus said he's coming back from heaven to save those that believe in him from all of the earthquakes and every other bad thing one day soon. Your old granddaddy may have to go meet Jesus before he comes here, but you will be here to see him when he comes in the sky on a great white cloud. He will come with all his angels and everything will be all right."

Little Timmy sat quietly listening and looked up at the big white clouds in the sky moving pass his grandfather's window.

Little Timmy turned his eyes back to his grandfather. He was waiting for him to say more. His grandfather put his hands on his shoulders, smiled and said, "Little Timmy son, no matter what happens in the world God is in control. When you are scared and don't know about something I want you to tell Jesus. He is always close by."

Little Timmy's grandfather then began to sing him a song: "He's got the whole world in his hands. He's got the whole wide world in his hands. He's got the whole world in his hands. He got the whole world in his hands."

Little Timmy's grandfather stretched out his big hands. Little Timmy laughed. His grandfather kept on singing:
"He's got me and your mother in his hands. He's got me and your mother in his hands. He's got me and your mother in his hands. He got the whole world in his hands."
"He got the little bitty baby in his hands . . ." Little Timmy's grandfather sang and sang. He only stopped to catch his breath every now and then.

Pastor Terrance Levise Turner, MBA
"The Earth Is Sad, Little Timmy"

About that time Little Timmy's parents came back with two nurses and said it was time to go. It had been a good long visit for Little Timmy's grandfather but it was time for him to take his medicine and rest. They all hugged and kissed him goodbye. Little Timmy's mother was the last to hug him goodbye. She put five pieces of butterscotch candy in his hand. He always liked butterscotch candy.
On the ride home, Little Timmy's father asked, "So little man what did your granddaddy and you talk about while we were away? Do you want to tell us about it?"
"We talked about earthquakes and Adam and Eve and how the earth is crying and about Jesus," Little Timmy said.
His father smiled and said, "Sounds like you had a lot to talk about son."

"We did Daddy," Little Timmy answered. Little Timmy then began to sing. "He's got the whole world in his hands. He's got the whole wide world in his hands. He's got the whole world in his hands. He got the whole world in his hands."
And Little Timmy sang and sang all the way home. His parents just smiled at one another they knew 'Granddaddy' had made it all right.

THE END

The Scientific Explanation Of Earthquakes

First of all, "What is an Earthquake?"

An earthquake is what happens when two giant slabs of the Earth's mantle underground moves past one another and gets hooked up on the edges creating a lot of energy to build up. The Earth moves along fault lines. A fault is a jagged line that separates these giant slabs of Earth underground.

When the earthquake is coming, sometimes a smaller earthquake will happen first before the big earthquake. The big earthquake is called the main earthquake. The main earthquake, which is very destructive, will usually be followed by smaller earthquakes that can also be very destructive. These smaller earthquakes can come days after the main earthquake, or even weeks after the main earthquake.

Why do we have earthquakes?

The earth itself has several layers. It has the inner core, outer core, the mantle, and the Earth's crust. Far underneath the ground that we see, are big slabs of the earth moving around, sliding past one another like a jigsaw puzzle. They move very slowly, but when they bump into one another they create a lot of energy. These large slabs of earth are called tectonic plates. The edges of these tectonic plates are the boundaries that get hooked up sometime when they slide past one another. These plate boundaries are at the same place where the fault lines are near the surface of the earth. This is where most earthquakes occur. When the edges of the plates get stuck, they will suddenly get unstuck and released a lot of energy. This is when we have earthquakes.

Earthquakes causes the Earth to "shake"

When energy is released from the tectonic plates that have been stuck together and suddenly moves and releases, it causes the energy to spread upward toward the surface of the Earth and shake the ground and everything on it where the fault lines are. It's like someone threw a rock in the middle of a pond and it made a big splash and the waves spread out over the whole pond. In an earthquake, these waves of energy are called seismic waves. Seismic waves move the Earth as they spread through it from the initial earthquake or movement at the site of the fault lines. When the waves reached the Earth's surface of the ground that we walk on everything on it moves and shakes. This is an earthquake.

How do we know how big an earthquake is?

Scientists measure earthquakes according to the size of the seismic waves. They use an instrument called a seismograph. The seismograph is a heavy instrument that hangs over a piece of paper like a pendulum and it shakes slightly according to the size of the earthquakes seismic waves and writes the waves on the piece of paper so that scientists can see how big the waves are for that particular earthquake. They can measure how big one earthquake's seismic waves were compared to another earthquake's seismic waves based on what the seismograph has written on the piece of paper.

Can we know if an earthquake is coming?

Pastor Terrance Levise Turner, MBA
"The Earth Is Sad, Little Timmy"

Sciences have not been able to specifically predict when an earthquake is coming. However, they can tell where earthquakes have been and may possibly come to in the future, based on where fault lines are in the earth. Fault lines our good indications of where an earthquake may come. The best thing that scientists and engineers can do is to try to build buildings, houses, bridges, and other structures strong and resilient enough to try to withstand the shaking of an earthquake when it does come. Human beings have been on the Earth for thousands of years, and God has protected us from earthquakes and many other natural disasters. God has allowed human beings and scientists to become smarter and smarter to find ways to help us survive even the unpredictable happenings, such as earthquakes. Ultimately, we are all dependent upon God, and He has the whole world in his hands. He will not let us go.

Salvation Prayer

Thank you for reading this book. I pray that it has blessed your life. I would like to give you the opportunity to know Jesus Christ as your Lord and Savior if you have not received Him into your heart. In the Bible, John 3:16–17 says,

For God so loved the world, that he gave his only begotten son, that whosoever believes in him should not perish, but have everlasting life. For God sent not his son into the world to condemn the world; but that the world through him might be saved.

If you have never received Jesus Christ as your Lord and Savior, I would like to lead you into a personal relationship with your Creator. He created you, and He planned your life from the beginning, before you ever entered the world. You were created by God. Yet, if you do not receive Jesus Christ as your Lord and Savior, you will never know God as your own personal Heavenly Father.

God gave the first man and woman, Adam and Eve, and instruction not to eat from the *tree of the knowledge of good and evil*. He said, if they ate from the tree, they would surely die. Well, tragically, Adam and Eve, the first man and woman, disobeyed God, and ate from the tree. When they did, they didn't die physically instantly. Yet, they did die spiritually. Their life with God, their Heavenly Father and Creator was cut off. They lost the nature of God. They lost the life of God. They lost relationship with God as their Father. He was still their Creator, yet the fatherly relationship had been tragically blocked by sin. They took on the nature of the one they allowed to deceive them, which was Satan. With Satan's nature in the earth, all of the fear, poverty, murder, hatred, deceit and destruction began to spread in the earth.

The only salvation for mankind was for God to send a Savior who did not have the nature of sin in His blood. That Savior was His own Son. God sent His only begotten Son, Jesus Christ, into the world to save mankind from the nature of sin. Jesus was born from a human mother who was a virgin. She had never been with a man. God supernaturally touched her womb and planted the seed of His Son in her womb so she could deliver Him into the world. His blood was free from the nature of sin. He was all man and yet all God. He was born from a physical woman, and from God's spiritual seed.

Jesus lived as a man on the earth. He lived free from sin. Yet he was tempted in all the ways, which we are tempted. Yet, through dependence on His God nature, He overcame every temptation. God, His Heavenly Father, helped Him to do that. Jesus fulfilled His destiny. His destiny was to be a sacrifice for you and me. He was crucified on the cross to pay for your sins and mine. He died in your place. This was His purpose for coming to the Earth. He came to restore you back into relationship with God as your Heavenly Father.

However, the only way to get back in your rightful position is to accept what Jesus did for you personally. Romans 10:9, 10, 13 has this to say:

That if you shall confess with your mouth the Lord Jesus as your Lord, and shall believe in your heart that God has raised him from the dead, then you shall be saved. With the heart man believe it unto righteousness; and with the mouth confession is made unto salvation. For whosoever shall call upon the name of the Lord shall be saved.

Therefore, it's just that simple. If you believe that Jesus is the Son of God and that He died in your place on the cross to pay for your sins, and that God raised Him from the dead for your victory;

then, the Bible says you will be saved. So now, just open your heart and open your mouth and repeat this prayer with me, now say,

    Dear Heavenly Father,

    I believe that Jesus is your only begotten Son. I believe that He came to die on the cross to pay for my sin to bring me back into relationship with you. I accept Jesus as my Lord and Savior. Jesus I call on you as my Savior. Jesus I accept you as my Lord. You have saved me and brought me back into relationship with God as my father. Thank you Lord Jesus. I am now born again. I now have eternal life with God in Heaven. Amen.

Now you are a son or daughter of God. You have been restored to your proper relationship with God. Now I want to encourage you to become a member of a church where you can grow in your relationship with God. Jesus wants to teach you how to live for Him. He is now your Shepherd and God. Now you will go through life knowing God as your Heavenly Father, and Jesus as Lord and Savior. God loves you. He will never leave you. He will be with you forever.

About The Author

Pastor Terrance Levise Turner, MBA is the Senior Pastor of Faith Country Holiness Church, in Gallatin, TN. Pastor Turner has an MBA in Finance and Supply Chain Management from Tennessee State University and a Bachelors degree in Mass Media from Tennessee State University. He is president of Well Spoken Inc., a media company, in Nashville, TN. Pastor Turner is the author of several books, including the **Distinguished Wisdom Presents . . ."Living Proverbs"** series, **Distinguished Wisdom Presents . . . Your Wealth Is In Your Anointing: Discover Keys To Releasing Your Potential**, **Distinguished Wisdom Presents . . . The Dynamic Victory Confession: Powerful Confessions For A Victorious Life**, **Distinguished Wisdom Presents . . . GAIN 20/20 VISION FOR THE NEW DECADE! A Step By Step Path To A More Successful Future**. For more information visit www.TerranceTurnerLivingProverbs.com. Or email WellSpokenInc@bellsouth.net. Pastor Turner is also a songwriter and recording artist with his wife, Dr. Avis Turner. He and his wife live in Nashville, TN.